Dear Parents and Educators,

Welcome to Penguin Young Readers! As pai [obscured by barcode] know that each child develops at his or her [obscured] speech, critical thinking, and, of course, reading. Penguin Young Readers recognizes this fact. As a result, each Penguin Young Readers book is assigned a traditional easy-to-read level (1–4) as well as a Guided Reading Level (A–P). Both of these systems will help you choose the right book for your child. Please refer to the back of each book for specific leveling information. Penguin Young Readers features esteemed authors and illustrators, stories about favorite characters, fascinating nonfiction, and more!

Ponies

LEVEL **2**

GUIDED READING LEVEL **I**

This book is perfect for a **Progressing Reader** who:
- can figure out unknown words by using picture and context clues;
- can recognize beginning, middle, and ending sounds;
- can make and confirm predictions about what will happen in the text; and
- can distinguish between fiction and nonfiction.

Here are some **activities** you can do during and after reading this book:
- Reading Comprehension: The author describes different ways in which ponies communicate. After reading the book, answer the following questions:
  - How do ponies greet one another?
  - How does a pony show that it is happy?
  - How do ponies make friends?
  - What does it mean when a pony rubs its nose against someone's cheek?
- Make Connections: Pretend you are the owner of a pony. Using the facts from this book, discuss how you would take care of your pony.

Remember, sharing the love of reading with a child is the best gift you can give!

—Bonnie Bader, EdM
   Penguin Young Readers program

*Penguin Young Readers are leveled by independent reviewers applying the standards developed by Irene Fountas and Gay Su Pinnell in *Matching Books to Readers: Using Leveled Books in Guided Reading*, Heinemann, 1999.

For Hiro Savage Kimura, cool colt—PP

For Sophie Margaret Sheehan—MB

To William, Nicole,
and a special thanks to Stefanie Z.—LB

Penguin Young Readers
Published by the Penguin Group
Penguin Group (USA) Inc., 375 Hudson Street, New York, New York 10014, USA
Penguin Group (Canada), 90 Eglinton Avenue East, Suite 700, Toronto, Ontario M4P 2Y3, Canada
(a division of Pearson Penguin Canada Inc.)
Penguin Books Ltd., 80 Strand, London WC2R 0RL, England
Penguin Group Ireland, 25 St. Stephen's Green, Dublin 2, Ireland (a division of Penguin Books Ltd.)
Penguin Group (Australia), 250 Camberwell Road, Camberwell, Victoria 3124, Australia
(a division of Pearson Australia Group Pty. Ltd.)
Penguin Books India Pvt. Ltd., 11 Community Centre, Panchsheel Park, New Delhi—110 017, India
Penguin Group (NZ), 67 Apollo Drive, Rosedale, Auckland 0632, New Zealand
(a division of Pearson New Zealand Ltd.)
Penguin Books (South Africa) (Pty.) Ltd., 24 Sturdee Avenue,
Rosebank, Johannesburg 2196, South Africa

Penguin Books Ltd., Registered Offices: 80 Strand, London WC2R 0RL, England

Text copyright © 2003 by Pam Pollack and Meg Belviso. Illustrations copyright © 2003
by Lisa Bonforte. All rights reserved. First published in 2003 by Grosset & Dunlap,
an imprint of Penguin Group (USA) Inc. Published in 2012 by Penguin Young Readers, an imprint of
Penguin Group (USA) Inc., 345 Hudson Street, New York, New York 10014. Manufactured in China.

Library of Congress Control Number: 2003004836

ISBN 978-0-448-42524-5   10 9 8 7 6 5 4 3 2 1

Ponies

by Pam Pollack and Meg Belviso
illustrated by Lisa Bonforte

Penguin Young Readers
An Imprint of Penguin Group (USA) Inc.

What's that on the hill?

It looks like a herd of baby horses.

But it is not.

It is a herd of ponies.

A pony looks like a horse.

But it is shorter.

That is what makes

it a pony.

A pony is never more

than 57 inches tall.

These ponies live on a farm.

The herd is like a family.

The head of the family is

the stallion.

The stallion protects

the other ponies.

They all work together.

The ponies in the herd

"talk" to each other.

One pony nickers.

That's how the ponies

greet one another.

The other pony blows

through his nose.

That shows he is happy.

A third pony flicks her tail.

What does that mean?

Nothing.

She is shooing away a fly.

Two ponies stand head to tail.

They pull their lips back.

They scratch each other's necks

with their teeth.

They are making friends.

A spotted pony stands apart.

Do you see how his ears are

pointed?

He is listening for something.

Ponies can hear things people

cannot.

A girl walks through the grass.

She is the pony's owner.

He is very happy to see her.

The pony runs to the fence.

He puts his nose out to be petted.

They go out riding.

She tells him where to go.

And she tells him how fast to go.

They start out walking.

Then they go faster.

They trot.

Walking and trotting

are called "gaits."

Cantering is a faster

gait than trotting.

Galloping is the fastest of all.

A pony can gallop

30 miles per hour.

People need a car to go that fast.

The girl leans forward.

She holds on tight.

Back on the farm,

the girl brings the pony

to his stall.

Caring for a pony is hard work.

Besides exercise,
a pony needs
lots of
fresh water
and hay.

He needs to be
brushed and
groomed.

His stall needs
to be cleaned.

Ponies get lonely by themselves. This pony's owner spends time with him every day.

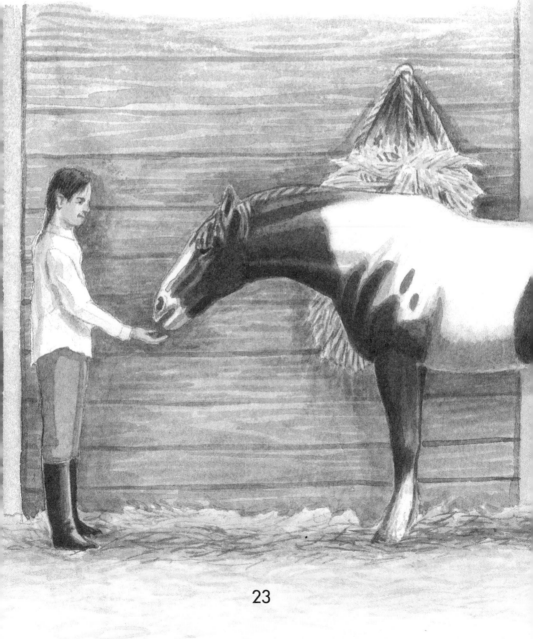

Ponies make good friends.

They like to have fun.

Sometimes they play jokes.

This pony has unlocked his stall.

His owner thinks that

she forgot to close it.

He does it again.

And again.

She laughs.

This time she knows

who did it.

One evening a baby pony is born.

A baby pony is called a foal.

His mother is called a mare.

An hour later,

he can already walk.

It is amazing.

newborn foal

foal at six months

full-grown pony

The foal stays close to his mother.

His mother watches out for him.

A pony is not full-grown

until it is five or six years old.

Ponies come in many colors.

They can be white, gray, brown,

red, golden, or black.

Some are a mix.

This pony has a
splash of white
between its eyes.
It is called a "star."

This pony has a line
down its face.
It is called a "stripe."

An extra-wide stripe
is called a "blaze."

32

The white part
here is called
a "stocking."

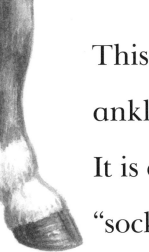

This pony's
ankle is white.
It is called a
"sock."

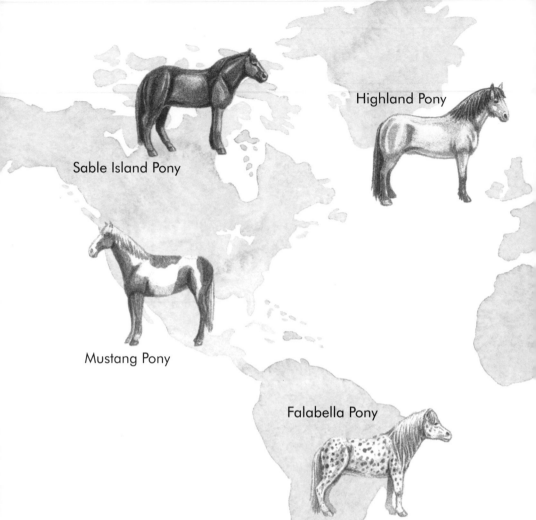

Highland Pony

Sable Island Pony

Mustang Pony

Falabella Pony

Ponies live all over the world.

There are ponies in

North and South America.

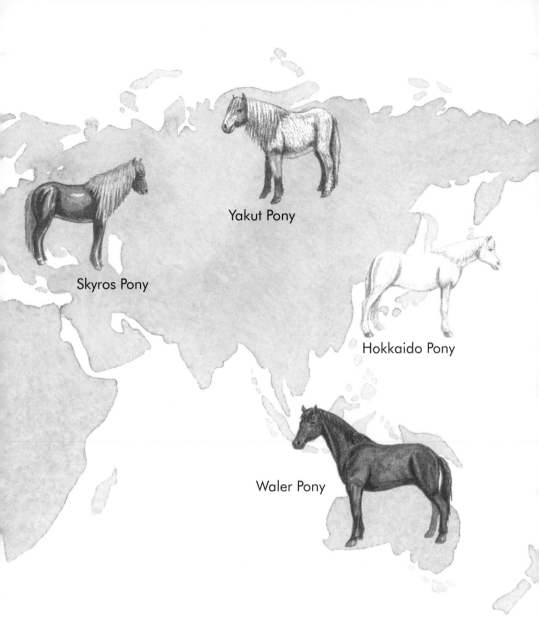

Yakut Pony

Skyros Pony

Hokkaido Pony

Waler Pony

There are ponies in Europe,
Asia, and Australia.

Most ponies live with people.

But some ponies live in the wild.

These wild ponies live

on a small island near Virginia.

The National Park Service

protects them.

Once a year, the ponies
are rounded up.
The ponies swim across
to another island.

It is called Chincoteague

(say: CHIN-ko-teeg).

People come from all over to watch.

A herd of wild ponies grazes

in a field.

Look! A bear is nearby.

One pony snorts.

That means danger.

Another pony roars.

That means, "Look out!"

The ponies run away

from the bear.

Even the foals can run very fast.

No one gets left behind.

They are all safe.

Wild ponies look out for

one another.

The sun is setting.

The wild ponies rest.

And on the farm,
the girl leads her pony
back to the barn.

The girl brushes him.

She washes his face.

She cleans his hooves.

She puts a blanket over him.

She scrubs his saddle.

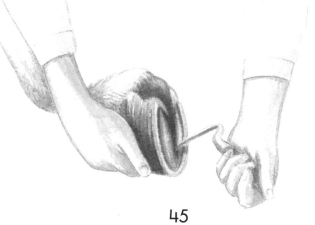

Now the pony is ready for bed.

His stall is filled with clean straw.

The straw is soft and dry.

The pony lies down.

He will have a nice, deep sleep.

"Good night, pony," the girl says.

She closes the stall door.

The pony rubs his nose

against her cheek.

That means, "I love you."

Tomorrow he will be ready

for more fun.